Running in the Dark is Nuts

NEIL GARROD

Copyright © 2024 Neil Garrod

All rights reserved.

ISBN: 979-88-7344-558-5

DEDICATION

To Natie

CONTENTS

	Acknowledgments	i
1	Silly Rhymes	3
2	The Solitary Runner	4
3	Bigots of the Tideway	5
4	Diluted Luddite	6
5	Courage	8
6	Not Wisdom but Info	9
7	Not Writing but Building	10
8	Good Grief	11
9	Bowled Over or Underbred?	12
10	Caroline Ellison Obituary (CEO)	14
11	Einstein Never Wore Socks	15
12	Che?	16
13	Cliché Consequence	17
14	Greet r (destiny), yo	18
15	I Believe	19
16	No Pavement Means Petition	20
17	Take the Pain	21
18	Sucked In	22

19	Transmogrify	23
20	Pleasure	24
21	Actions Speak Louder than Words	25
22	Puppies in a Gunny Sack	26
23	L***	27
24	Na Nana Na Na	28
25	Valiant Levant	29
26	Where Every Shade of Grey Has a Name	31
27	Revolution	32
28	Return and Repeat	33
29	What Did the Romans Ever do For Us?	34
30	Age of Enlightenment	36
31	Fibonacci's Respect	39
32	Karen	40
33	One Lump or Two?	42
34	Ubi Nihil Valis, Ibi Nihil Velis	43
35	Impotent	44
36	Incontinence Blues	45
37	Eunuch	46
38	Early Morning Prostrate Blues	47

39	Last Candles	48
40	Pont yr Achub	49
41	Pronouns	50
42	Life	51
43	Plain Jane	52
44	Parallax Rocks Parallel	53
45	Refraction	54
46	Rising Man	55
47	Successful Mediocrity	56
48	Nemo Me Impune Lacessit	57
49	Autumn Glows	59
50	Gravity Just a Second Thought	60
51	Four Times of the Day	61
52	Sometimes the Rage Bites Hard	62
53	Dressed Stone	68
54	Friendship	69
55	Folded Parchment	70
56	Freedom	72
57	Bud, Bloom and Blossom	74
58	Evensong	75

59	Too Many Notes	77
60	Muzak	78
61	Struck Dumb	79
62	Hush	80
63	Two or One	81
64	Unrequited	82
65	Com'è Profondo il Mare	83
66	Bill Got the Lyrics Right	84
67	Labour Lea	85
68	Public Transport	86
69	Now	87
70	We Two	88
71	Touch	89
72	Madres Paralelas	90
73	Angus	91
74	Forever Further Down the Road	92
75	Take Your Coat Off or You Won't Feel the Benefit	94
76	Graded Grains Make Finer Flour	95
77	I'm Sorry But I Don't Apologise	96
78	Odour of Self Righteousness	97

79	But What Does it Mean?	98
80	White Horses	99
81	Rent in Pieces	102
82	Blind Reaper	103
83	Told You So	104
84	Learn to Take Yes for an Answer	105
85	Reverse to Reserve	107
86	Bedtime Grime	108
87	Corporate Rot	109
88	Just One for the Road	110
89	End of the Road	111
90	Indegism	112
91	Crescent Moon	113
92	Journey	114
93	Crossing Lines	115
94	Emigré	116
95	Amazing Men	117
96	County Down	118
97	Dangerman	119
98	Sail before Steam	121

99	Harbour Lights	125
100	Searching	126
101	Inside Out	127
102	Morituri te Salutant	128
103	Running in the Dark	130

ACKNOWLEDGMENTS

To Natie's 50th birthday for setting me on this road
To Michelle for the idea of a book for the 50th birthday
To Natie for being 50 and for his never dying encouragement
To Sonja Gortnar for the portrait of me on the book cover, along with so much, much more

4 Diluted Luddite: to George Bilgere via Diane Lockward for the idea

6 Not Wisdom but Info and 7 Not Writing but Building: with due deference and admiration to Stevie Smith

8 Good Grief: to and for Gill Emmanuel

14 Greet r (destiny), yo: ode to Breaking Bad

29 What Did the Romans Ever do For Us?: with due deference and admiration to Monty Python

43 Plain Jane: with due deference and admiration to Philip Larkin

51 Four Times of the Day: Jean-Baptiste-Camille Corot inspired these thoughts

49 Autumn Glows and 102 Harbour Lights: with due deference and admiration to Dylan Thomas

1. Silly Rhymes

If odes get heavy and just too glum
It's time to lighten, write something dumb
Best still with rhyme and jaunty prose
Where meter always leads our nose

The problem is when drafting rhyme
Thoughts rush back to nursery time
So dull, so sparse, so non descript
More fun to have your toe nails clipped

But there I go with morbid thoughts
Why can't I stick to sunny ports?
Don't know, don't care, I have no need
Because, in fact, not of that creed.

August 2021

Neil Garrod

2. The Solitary Runner

The hour is small
The day newborn

Sky still with heavy lids
Blinks sullen drowsy eyes

Meanders smooth and resting still
Uncut, unscathed by scull or oar

Street lights confused go each their shaded way
Few still shine, some blink, whilst more now slumber

Goblets of dew sit plump and bold on giving leaves
Blackbirds bustle, doves coo and preen and gild their troth

The homeless rise and smile their once that day
To tidy junk of others in their nest

Time for solitary runners
Who worship, take and spoil in one

Yet soundly sleep each night
In certain ken all will

Return next day
Rehearsed, refreshed

May 2021

3. Bigots of the Tideway

The river flows, the sea fights back
Bedfellows sharing top to toe
Two forces blind to their own lack

Long lost cousins from same egg sac
Moonstruck siblings that each don't know
The river flows, the sea fights back

What might begin as full attack
Soon drains away to something faux
Two forces blind to their own lack

Fresh water cleans away the plaque
Returned as salted guano
The river flows, the sea fights back

Dispositions back-to-back
That rage and calm blow-by-blow
Two forces blind to their own lack

Flood and current flex six pack
Slack water more like saggy dough
The river flows, the sea fights back
Two forces blind to their own lack

November 2021

4. Diluted Luddite

Poems too imagined for computer world
Or so we are enjoined
No rhyme, no ode, no lyricism
Harsh words only for this modernism
Artist's sketchpad, the great entreat
Sumptuous, no less, than 8 by10
Accompanied by a nice gel pen

I love the pen, I love the pad
I love the disconnect off grid
But my grind needs helping tools
And not just mere romantic rules

Passioned odes enough for me
Voyeurs on sensuality
So start with simple
Just £1 pad
That fits old leather writing case
Worn and battered with history
Plus pencil, no ink based sophistry

A fountain pen a magic quill
Reserved for final finished will
Or sought and hefty moniker
But not for drafts or chronicler

Yet leaded scrawlings in the pad
Need discipline and stylish pout
To finish, for their coming out

Running in the Dark is Nuts

Typewriter would be just perverse
So laptop keyboard it must be
And see how scales then rise and fall
With screen and keyboard in a dance
That lets the words and lines chassé
To unknown place, choreography

Sometimes to check, sometimes just try
Great lines, in need of pruning shears
Great lines, in need of graft elsewhere
Great lines, that have no bed just here
Propagate with cut and paste
Bad lines, deserving no repeat
Delete, delete, delete, delete

No, George, you are mistook
For some of us the laptop is
Our foetal membrane chord
Between our frenzied ruminations
And calligraphic revelations

February 2022

5. Courage

Age would give me coeur
Age would give me heart
Unformed in one so young
Where growth presumed
But heart does not assume
Turns out an ageless gift
Set at birth
How sad for us more timid

May 2023

6. Not Wisdom but Info

His message unsent, no signal,
Debate still in limbo:
His thirst only quenched by a tablet
Not with wisdom but info.

Poor chap, he always loved learning
So many views
It must have been too much for him his brain gave way,
Fake news.

Oh, no no no, there was too much always
(Often said to our hero)
He was much too thirsty all his life
But for wisdom not info.

February 2023

Neil Garrod

7. Not Writing but Building

Nobody heard him, the writer,
But still he wrote pending:
I was much deeper in than you thought
And not writing but building.

Good chap, he always loved learning
Never brain dead
The BE was switched for BA, white privilege
They said.

Oh, no, no no it was writing always
(Writing with brick and not pen)
I was much too in concrete not paper
And not building but writing.

16th June 2023

8. Good Grief

An oxymoron term for Charlie's peanut crush
As now I think of you.
Detention Marge, you only asked the way
Or was it for the time?
Small point, as Homer knew he'd overstepped
Missed golden chance apology set straight.
Starting numb, so they say, the chaos leads to order
Our memories, not tagged and clean, bring pain as well as wonder
For you, for me, that cooking sherry almost broke the camel
But you, dab hand in two faced childs, made sure there was no trammel
Matthew 5 sub section 4, beatitude for twins
Who look both ways so need a guide and favoured if we find
    A few of us have luck in spades to get a two in one
        You and me linked through him, a trinity bar none.

13.12.22

for 12.12.22

9. Bowled Over or Underbred?

Un petit cadeaux
The source of the name
for the day that runs after
unorthodox Christmas.

Box
A pretty word
Short and crisp
Unloved by ears
Deceptive in its sound
Imprisoning in its stealth
With gilded chains
That lock
And cut the air
That stops the breath
Preventing growth
Hors d'oeuvre to
Selfish nibble
That lets us know ourselves
Until we disappear and
Let others claim
Posthumous fame
In our name.

So they may seem
uncornered in their view
A blame passed on

Running in the Dark is Nuts

to broad yet drooping shoulders
set firm in aspic
that has no future
and possibly no past.
More emperor's clothes
dry cleaned to give shape,
yet still no form to coat a hangar.

Hung in colour code
by length as well
so that the box may be machined
to size that fits
us all,
if we don't mind a popping seam
half mast legs or armpit waist.
Trés chic, they all proclaim
(all children banned to silent room)
and so
we can,
with knowing sigh,
get lost amongst the ornate carving on
the well shaped box
disguising precious gift within.

February 2023

10. Caroline Ellison Obituary (CEO)

Profit and loss squeezed
To P and L
To P&L
To pnl
Crypto speak for
Present not loan:
SBF's effective altruism

October 2023

11. Einstein Never Wore Socks

Einstein or Zweistein
One brain or two
They say more is better
But just for the few

Some of us struggle
And want a bit more
It's said to be greedy
We're meant to be poor

Well, bollocks to that
If you'll excuse the profane
Self righteous can get stuffed
We're all built the same

Some are just lucky
Three presents at birth
Some are just short changed
No heaven on earth

Compare and contrast
On lucky and earned
Just think of the sockless
They're not to be spurned

Boxing Day 2023

12. Ché?

But what is the question?
Knowledge unknown
The frame squares the answer
Standing or prone

What we don't know
Itself an unknown
Until we name it
And give flesh and bone

Questions not floating,
Particles unknown,
Sculpted and chiseled
By things that are known

True questions themselves
Part of the unknown
So how can we ask them
Before our gravestone

September 2023

13. Cliché Consequence

Connected clichés, you know the ones:
America sneezes the World catches cold.
Middlebrow dinner chat makes us feel learnèd
But learning needs thinking, all absent here
Vacuous statements for vacuous chats
Eyes bigger than stomach bite more than can chew
Clichés just pour out, cheeks puffed with dross
Statements of mocking that others don't hear

So easy to scoff, less easy to swallow
As usual some truth in grandpa's wife's tale:
Butterfly wings and ripples on pond
Always go somewhere far and beyond
Our actions designed to impact close to
But we have no sanction on where they will end
Hubris and blindness and crass just don't care
Always assume unasked consequence rare
But ripples do travel with infinite life
Be careful what wished for
Dreams can be gutted with blunt butter knife

July 2023

Neil Garrod

14. Greet r (destiny), yo

Hope's sweet dreams bud with promised fruit
Fed by sun and showers that swell the fragile crop of pride
Burned by chill of cowardice
Leaves futures bone gnawed barren

Black dog teeth remuzzled by hard wire
Adopted fallen petals scent Geppetto's son
To lead him by the nose that scars his face
And balks that most precious kiss of all

Camel straw sucks up last remaining hope
Toilet water sent to long drop stench
That festers round the deep black hole
Where stars all shot to death and heavens die

Or not. Regret still sits with rules all now rewrit
Recaste, rescind. Socio shrinks to psycho
Medicated by the family balm
Bedazzled by the shimmering new born prize

For it's not him this time, all others are to blame
Collateral damage and friendly fire
Euphamistic anaesthetics that numb all pain
As he is due, the world to see him as he should have formed

New him, begat in lust by regret,
Reborn from despair, suckled by freedom
That's just another word for nothing else to lose
Except his soul
That consumes itself in its white heat of fame

November 2021

15. I Believe

Two words, three syllables
All it takes to conjure miracles
That rip the heart from any sense
But transform history to future tense
The zealot claims it's life affirming
Thomas claims it's life constricting
Both believing yet not proving
Just one dismissing the other choosing

October 2022

Neil Garrod

16. No Pavement Means Petition

The gentle folk of Chiswick Mall stroll out in dappled shade
They push their babes and walk their dogs on manicured macadam
Between their piles and Thames side greens possessed by fine clipped hedge
The Mall reclines, a cultured place awaiting genteel passage
It sports a gracious footway path flagged in Yorkshire stone
A peaceful, tranquil, dream like place not known for rowdy scenes
Until exclusive rights proclaimed by ambulatory folk
They walk and push and preen and jog right down the cambered crown
The pavement shunned and left renounced by those for whom constructed
So cars and bikes must slalom through rule breaking local peds
The honk of horn and ding of bell informs of faulty useage
But strollers of the Chiswick Mall just turn and wonder why
There's transport of the round wheeled kind on their beloved turf
Neither bunch can understand what is the other's problem
The glares are fierce from both cohorts, their questions, both the same,
Remain unasked, no answer sought, "why are you in my space?"
Sometimes some words can be exchanged, not pleasant ones at all
The transport crew can quote the book, the hallowed Highway Code
Whilst ambulators feel a right most sacred, self bestowed
Seems strange to me that both sides feel that god is on their side
With justice weeping scales of doubt, no bartered give and take
As rules is rules and all should know they're written to the letter
So why do those who stroll and live in general by the book
Ignore the code in their domain, the Thames path pilgrim's way
Glut of privilege must play its part but also people power
When most agree no rule makes sense their acts can change the zeitgeist
But still one feels with some unease the rightness of their cause
For be assured, without a doubt no pavement means petition

August 2023

17. Take the Pain

To be human is to be wrong
To be wrong is to be chastised
To be chastised is to be sad
To be sad is to be thoughtful
To be thoughtful is to be human

April 2023

18. Sucked In

Probably not envisaged route
Doubtless not even planned
No maps, no signs, the course unmarked
A way not even seen

But current lures in just one way
A pull not lunar led
So where's it from, this hidden force
That sucks on milkless teat

Once in the stream go with the flow
As if had come from source
Act as if it was forethought
A rational woven thread

Warp or weft, no way to tell
A weave not of your own
So better still confess no clue
Sucked in, spat out, not you

July 2023

19. Transmogrify

The fishers come home
Below their catch, above birds
A seething white foam

May 1968

Neil Garrod

20. Pleasure

To please or be pleased?
The fact that you ask makes clear
Sadly it's neither

August 2023

21. Actions Speak Louder than Words

Gusset, crotch and damp
Tragic words to quell the joy
Moistly heaven sent

June 2023

Neil Garrod

22. Puppies in a Gunny Sack

Thought uncool to stare these days
but jumping pups rekindle sap
long sluggish, lost and with no map
to memory that shimmers in the haze
of long past youth, of lust that's
still not dead so grateful for
the Jerry's fretted finger chords
that strengthen any crumbling husk.
But let's not brood on crusted angst
Give thanks for canines' frisky
visions sweet in current times
Be sure, and always, nought else ranks

September 2021

23. L***

Lust has had bad press these days
A victim of hash tag, peut être
Now prancing love is centre stage
Much softer, milder
Metaphysical guage

Lust is earthy, plain and simple
Feelings driving without consent
Rushing juices out in costume
Blinding eyes, redoubling touch
Each scent and odour erotic perfume

Loves confusing, Irish signposts
Lilting passion, empty goodbye
Fig leaf to my carnal world
Where lust one way, a direct road
No ifs no buts all banners unfurled

Cupid's quiver full of arrows
Tipped with lust no love in sight
No aim, no target, all ricochet
Right from my heart to
Unknown prey

So less of the foreplay
Get straight to the point
Love blossoms with time
But only with kick start
From loins, yours and mine

December 2023

24. Na Nana Na Na

Tit for tat
A childish ploy
That soon enough
Can grow up to
Rat a tat

From gawky youth
To ugly age
Shooting through
The elegance
Of maturity
Taking breath
In battle field
A hesitance revealed
Inhaled as coward's choice
Pure mamby pamby

Yet jaw, jaw, jaw
Not war, war, war
Can play its part
In absence of
Blah, blah, blah

October 2023

25. Valiant Levant

Pale stain is real
Pleasantries lie

Strange to say it all depends on
Tongues and lips and mouth
Those golden sounds made with no touch:
a, e, i, o, u
Even more, just one, two, three
Drive the hidden sense
No eye for eye
But a for e
Turns vessels into vassals
Then make the change
And mix them up
And Levant grows more valiant.

Then, aye aye, a single switch turns
Palestine to pale stain
Or make no change
Just flip them round
And Israël is real

If the ayes take the day
And have it in their hands
Pale flips to pail
Which, in its turn,
Losses all
Significance

Neil Garrod

As cargo vessel
Navigates
Round and round and round
To spew its load
As number one
To rationalise the vassal

Anagrams mix things up
And make us all confused
As raga man plays sitar
Airts point in new direction

Spellings change
Language yields
The kernel's just the same
So tell that to the colonels on
The Levant battlefields.

October 2023

26. Where Every Shade of Grey Has a Name

Raised to the power by binary clout
Electrons spin round from zero to one
Circling the life flame like laagering wagons
Defending what's in and keeping what's out

Tides pull the alga as moon beats the rhythm
Predicting the right way with strictest precision
No nuance or doubt, the model is god
No lunacy suffered through this special prism

Systems of colour manage the flow
Red warns of danger, no sense to proceed
Green lures with earnest, go forward with speed
Yellow has meaning more hazy and mellow

Prime yellow's in doubt, unsure of her stance
Listens to others with wide open bearing
Reviled, as an upshot, for lacking in sureness
Rejecting both dogmas to revel in nuance

Colours are coded in circular wheels
Primary antithesis to complimentary
Mix them together get some sort of grey
Now life becomes subtle, probing ideals
Shades are mysterious, nothing is tamed
That's where we are now, we don't know our place
So mould and reshape a new colour scheme
Where all shades of grey are baptized and named

March 2022

Neil Garrod

27. Revolution

Protestors hosed with cannon
dry their wings like shags
caught out mid cycle
by marauding scum
forced into their inner space
that can't be cleansed
by any spurt of Adam's
ale meant for succour
not for holy inquisition
that purges doubt from all
their minds with strict precision
of the guided jet
that whittles down creator's nous
to common shredded pulp
in face of what the fellowship
knows is best visage
for every dross
with any spunk
to speak their mind in face
of brutish or benign intransigence
and spawn the wave that in its turn
does wash the sacred cannon clean

Ulysses, Candlemas, Groundhog Day 2022

28. Return and Repeat

Living your life, ignore my perception
Two of your wrongs don't make me a right
But lets not get forward your free will a joke
Not costless but binding in any law court
Irrevocable choices now set in stone
Changes are future not a back date
Honing and moulding what some call our fate
Not written in tablets but ours to dictate

Nurture and nature the luck of the draw
No time travel options to change what has been
So why do we do it, look over our shoulder
Mistakes of our past just make us feel older
Best look to the future our only true freedom
To alter our steering, our personal Te Deum

360 vision shows context not choice
Ruts sinking in history, engrained here and after
Laid out in confusion with perfect foresight
Like so many fillets on fishmongers' slab
That given the choice select their own rank
On pristine white marble, their known catafalque

January 2023

Neil Garrod

29. What Did the Romans Ever do For Us?

Injustice is the greatest crime
Apart from all the others
A system forced on to a mess
Held close by local grime

Clean out that mess the purists cry
Let's make things spick and span
Perfection rests in logic thought
Not in a local lie

How little heed is given to
The warts in perfect scheme
All overlooked by practised eye
And specs of pinkish hue

The specks upon our kitchen floor
Stay camouflaged to us
Within this smog our plans take form
A framework for our core

Not all bodies made the same
Bones shaped by local lens
Eyesight trimmed by blinkered heart
Perfection hobbled lame

Emperor's clothes seen from afar
Hide no local shame
But form a flag to which we run
Our bright and burnished star

Running in the Dark is Nuts

Worn at home they fit their role
Howlers not withstanding
Passed on to those who seem unclothed
They show up every hole

It seems that their own grubby rags
Hold style for their own form
They fit just right, whilst in our clothes
They look like wretched scumbags

September 2023

30. Age of Enlightenment

To document
To box our lives
To prove a point
To bring hard fact
To self expression
An ugly act

All our lives
Now documented
Births and first school days
Weddings and graveyard scene
And worst of all, fun
Betwixt and between

Not like before
When memory was
Sole recall
On which to base
Sweet recollections
Stories embrace

Memories gathered
Stories moulded
Stuck together
As we recall
Ensuring beauty
For us and all

Perception rules
Or maybe timing
Life not tickbox or
Evidence based
Memories revisioned
Original cut paste

Rule of the doc
Shaped by the wants
Of others who judge
What said and we did
Not how we recall
But through camera's eyelid

Why would we tell
An ugly tale?
Tumbling down
Happy and drunk:
A story to tell,
A photo to junk

Photograph fixes
All things in time
The ugly and beauty
All that has been
Except, we are missing
Nowhere to be seen

Captured in shot
But lacking in freedom
Kris hit the jackpot
When got Bobby to say
It's all about assets
None left to mislay

Also it means
The chance to portray
Life as we want it
It's in the deception
That freedom finds
Immaculate conception

Neil Garrod

Mirrors can save us
Show what is needed
A photo to others
For us, more aloof.
Everyone's happy
But just I know the truth

January 2024

31. Fibonacci's Respect

A
Home
Castle
Moated place
A crafted nest to
Eat, sleep, read and love. To share with
All, secure as turtle doves that twigs protect intact
In our design, not tweaked nor twitched by beaks that then fly on to their own inviolate coop.

July 2021

32. Karen

Shame that for some of us labels come early
That pesky Y chrome upsetting the wish
And so the planned Karen cut down to a Neil
Two consonants discarded and first vowel too
Replaced with some others, an alpahabet coup

NB, for the record, important to note
This Karen was wished for some L years before
Her name stole and tarnished by twitter brigade
The wish was for XY to balance two Xs
Not demanding, entitled, but clearly still vexes

Families are havens so must be a joke
But feelings are stumped in first ever over
Pavilioned in humour in own bell size jar
I thinks as I listen that I'm noticed at last
But deep down I know I'm just an outcast

A stand in, offender, supplanter of what?
Tricky to answer not wearing that hat
I know nothing other, must do what I can
A light hearted joke that I get not at all
So step all too lightly and try not to fall

I never wore dresses, make up or heels
But some things much better if left unsaid
Disappointment from outset tricky to lose
These days I'd be counseled, cherished and humoured
Those days quite different, or so it is rumoured

That set the scene for the fumbles to come
Striking the high notes with tremulous doubt
That sanctify falsehoods running rings round the truth
If only the ref declared technical knock out
Life might have seemed a less unequal bout

December 2022

33. One Lump or Two?

One ball sack:
Half full or half empty?
Man lite or eunuch heavy?
The Hitler club none keen to join
Membership just for singles
But numbers keep growing
Genes striding the void
Protection essential
Against goose step foot
Low fist or sudden head butt.
One starts to wonder
Why most bother with two
Twice the weight and twice the space
Sounds inefficient
Just an insurance
That makes no good sense
'Til things are deficient.
For those of you hung
With one on both sides
Lopsiders thank for your care
We recognise the sacrifice
From carrying that built in spare.

September 2023

34. Ubi Nihil Valis, Ibi Nihil Velis

Never thought that made a circle
But here we are again
Feeling only truth
First used to celebrate
To show the cerebral
But now, full circle
It eats away at inner frame
Built through time
Demolished in a stroke
Of hubris doubt
A hewn out shell
That only I can see
All others snowed by emperor flakes
As jaws drop south
To see the castle built on sand
Sink beneath

May 2023

Neil Garrod

35. Impotent

Ever journey, no arrive
Orchestra full, empty play
Tension rises, slips away
Left lying flat, no revive

March 2023

36. Incontinence Blues

Cheeks compressed, the walking stilted
Guts in revolt and pained
Inside alive but outwardly
Everything constrained

Set out with joy the amble planned
The view could not be faulted
Yet now the pain takes all away
A shit that can't be halted

A part of life controlled before
Now dominates all pleasure
Attempts to rule don't work at all
Uncontrollable pressure

I cut it fine, but much too fine
Oh no, what a disaster
I guessed it wrong, the walking brought
Things forward so much faster

Finally I understand
I have no power or glory
A fiction never visualised
A shit show type of story

August 2023

37. Eunuch

A view not seen
A sound not heard
An angle thought straight
So never drawn

March 2023

38. Early Morning Prostrate Blues

 "Good morning, we are so thankful for
Your valued custom" voice so brash and bold
"May I, please, for just a sec, put you on hold?"
No sir, no way, no thank you
The time to wait is still not come
Not now with misting breath like morning dew
So get a grip and flip that answer switch
You wet my bed, you crimped my sheets, you sired my bouncing babes
With such surprising ease when some restraint, delay
Would likely been so well received
So now your new found hesitance is rich
I know just me on hold, to moan and bitch
       But still, let go you bastard, let that morning stream
       So I can leave these cold floor tiles and shuffle back to dream

November 2021

Neil Garrod

39. Last Candles

Soixante neuf can raise an eyebrow
Gorged with Gallic innuendo
C'est ooh là là from top to toe
A double entendre that some avow

Sixty nine, on other hand,
So very Anglo Saxon
Dreary count from natal day
Three score and ten the one next planned

Which some would say is our end game
And this, indeed, might be my fate
But some have passed Go more than once
And claim ten sevens just not the same

That fêted anniversary
They say should not be numbered
Post 69 there is no count
No need for age based perjury

Psalms 90:10 revoked with glee
The magic number bettered
So 69 is final time
For candles at the birthday tea

From now on in the 7th of June
Is just a celebration
No adding up or counting back
Arithmetic inopportune

7th June 2023

40. Pont yr Achub

Bridges bipolar, not sure where to stand
One foot or other or just lend a hand
Some bridges call you to cross and return
Some just for one way, designed so can burn
Sometimes they bond, sometimes separate
A toll bridge, oxymoron, unless to escape
They form and they save when slippery slope
Take me to new lands full of green hope
So many bridges crossed without note
Not seeing their reach keeps my head afloat
Crossing their arches, eyes in the shade
No thanks, no awareness, no gratitude paid
    Now it is different, unblinkered I see
    They took me to new ground that found only me

March 2022

Neil Garrod

41. Pronouns

My skill at sums peaked in binary
Linear led me to zero one
For me, the best was always constrained
For crunchers and reckoners, their language untamed
A method of blinking and passing the message
Frowned on these days but winking works well
Outside to calm us, the lights off and on
Inside they're working, circling electron

In the days of my youth a specialist field
These days the binary a language of all
Him, her and them
Or maybe we're all wrong
No binary here
Looks much more like ternary, end points with space
Pronouns, let's face it, not beautiful sounds
No Maria in hiding in those harsh tone mounds

So let me divert for a second or two
We all can be victims in naming roulette
I was to be Karen but the Xs too few
With luck I sit comfy with substitute choice
Neil does just fine and gives me my voice

So choose your own pronoun, I'll pay it due deference
Just remember your name is my personal preference

January 2022

42. Life

File the anagram under meaning unknown
A hot air balloon that lifts out of sight
Till heat is all gone and air dissipates
A black hole of nothing disowned by the fates

Once there was future now it's all past
Age not the issue, nor the constraint
As ballast ejected time to see clear
Was only the striving that kept the veneer

Time to reflect is a wonderful thing
To nibble and snack during ascension
Autosarcophagy a healthy distraction
Until it becomes the only abstraction

Rising and rising the ground fades away
Horizons grow wider, boundaries not cramped
Until there is nothing, confusion abounds
All hot air now literal, the vacuum astounds

Black holes suck all in, or that's what they claimed
Now doubt as some leaks found, power released
Reflection seems pointless but then turn around
The mirror's more honest, a life to nail down

Burn's night January 2023

43. Plain Jane

She walks life unnoticed
Not heard nor even seen
A sphincter moving on her own
Floating on no one's cloud

Someone that doesn't trouble
The space in others' minds
Silent footsteps strike no slabs
She barely takes a breath

Larkin's bud as yet unfurled
May flower in many ways
He wishes her the ordinary
Or better still the dull

Walking silent leaves her free
To blossom in her way
Without the gusts from windy day
And absent others' say

August 2023

44. Parallax Rocks Parallel

Two letters from eight is all that it takes
One vowel, one consonant turns certain to fake
Straight vision turns sideways, black shades to white
Acute and obtuse can all look quite right

Rabbits from top hats like magic appear
To hip and to hop and scurry with fear
This way and that way, who knows which is best
When ley lines turn crooked and dreams come to rest

Where curves ironed flat and irons take flight
As el turns to ax, day turns to night
Your truth is my lie, I just cannot see
Nothing but woods, not one single tree

December 2021

Neil Garrod

45. Refraction

Mirror man mirror me as others see my soul
As voices warp when they're played back
So mirrors hide our truth
Not Dorian deep but more profound
A parallel imperception

We know ourselves,
Ho ho to that,
But others may not see
Yet, then again, perception's all
Self knowledge contraception

'Take or leave', the narcist cry
Unfair to all the rest
Their image set, when truth be told,
Reflecting on the other view
May add a new dimension

The Captain's words never meant so much
As now when they're most needed
Before was just a crazy tune
That precious few respected
Yet needed close attention

If he can make us more reflect
Then benefit for all
To see ourselves as others do
Might save us from the worst of all
Unchallenged self deception

Burn's night January 2023

46. Rising Man

Dough has to prove itself time after time
Me I'm more touchy and find it a grind
My choices are mine no need to debate
With some being stupid and some rather great
Ex post analyses do not make them better
Simply enrage and make differences fester
Review of a choice good for the future
But backwards critique no current suture
Critique is so sloppy when phrased in the past
Helpful is something applied that can last
Bickering and pointing with fingers so long
Can only bring downfall no victory song
      Back peddle on past to push things more forward
      Eye on the future makes things more straightforward

September 2023

Neil Garrod

47. Successful Mediocrity

Genius never, ever quite enough
A pot of gold at rainbow's end
That lurches and bobbles just out of sight
Never so distant to never leave marks
Never so current to burn all the sparks

A teasing coquette that knows both the limits
To keep me enraptured yet not satisfied
Playing with substance as well as the gaps
I think I might leave her but she knows the score
Never too little I always want more

Try counting back from the last time the lack
Smothered the pleasure of where I'd arrived
Struggling and sweating I got to my top
Knowing I'd reached so much higher than before
In plain sight of summit, those few metres more

Plain, rationed victuals are all I can stomach
Rich food that's craved not meant for my palette
How often I've tried, just suffering gut ache,
So back to the usual left overs restaurant
For sandwich of fear between hubris and want

St. Swithin's Day, July 2023

48. Nemo Me Impune Lacessit

I

Lowly creeping common weed
Radar trap for Nordic kings
Regal raiment in its flower
Tender fragrance in its scent
So much sweeter in their acres
Noble bloom of royal hue
Spectacle in wind swept masse
Glinting winged as dragonfly
And when those glory days passed by
Seeds sustain a throng
Gold and greenfinch, redpoll, linnet
Gorging in the spiky larder
    Replete and sated they still return
    For bedding for their nesting arbour

II

Lowly creeping common weed
Radar trap for Nordic kings
Regal raiment in its flower
Tender fragrance in its scent
Spectacle in wind swept masse
Glinting winged as dragonfly
And when those glory days passed by
Seeds sustain a throng
Gold and greenfinch, redpoll, linnet
Gorging in the spiky larder
Replete and sated they still return
For bedding for their nesting arbour
    Grandeur comes in many forms
    Not all fitting standard norms

III

Lowly creeping common weed
Radar trap for Nordic kings
Regal raiment in its flower
Tender fragrance in its bower

So much sweeter in their acres
Noble bloom of royal hue
Spectacle in wind swept sky
Glinting winged as dragonfly

When those glory days passed by
Seeds sustain a throng
Redpoll, linnet, finches gold and green
Gorging in the spiked canteen

Replete and sated they still return
For bedding for their nesting arbour
Grandeur comes in many forms
Not all fitting standard norms

September 2023

49. Autumn Glows

Swallows wired in next high caper
Starlings murmur admiration
Robins find their voice reclothed
Apples bramley, brambles plumpen
Timid plums flush puce to sweeten
Harvest baskets, larders bursting
Herald time for some's Thanksgiving

Yet mood is on the turn
As roaving scythes lay ripened ears to husk
Bulbs switch off their bedside lamp
Awaiting increased tog to keep them cosy
Street lamps flicker out of short time working
Casting neon shades on russet leaves
That rage against the dying of the light

Sun swings just one leg from its bed
Hour hand, exhausted, strains with dew
Until, no longer, it falls back
And thick grey clouds protect from God's Personal Sight

September 2021

Neil Garrod

50. Gravity Just a Second Thought

Plump, ripe orb
Too heavy for its wombing chord
Falls down to feed, return, rebirth
And in that moment when it strikes
It's earthly home, it's life, full turn
Presents and speaks two seasons full of work
Climaxed, wearied, satisfied

All the rain and sun long round
All wild bee courtship, spring flower dances
All bird and human voices playing summer branches
Caught, revealed and cherished in a single sound

Words weave sounds to human warp
Filled by Autumn weft
But onomatopoeia fails this time
Drump, per donk, bomp, thunk do not suffice
Release the sound itself to make its voice

In repose young Isaac sees the russet fall
And hears the no word heavenly chord
That spoke to him as us all
And woke him from his reverie
To ground himself in Newton's
Simpler land based gravity

September 2021

51. Four Times of the Day

In around 1858, Jean-Baptiste-Camille Corot was commissioned by his friend and fellow artist Alexandre Gabriel Decamps (1803–1860) to paint panels depicting four times of day. He chose Morning, Noon, Evening and Night. They hang in the National Gallery in London.

I chose four different measures of the day for my four Haikus

Dawn

Infinite promise
Safely delivered on time
In so many ways

Forenoon

Sun now being up
Day can begin in earnest
With no seeming end

Afternoon

Siesta your choice
Indolent time whatever
Fall with no colour

Dusk

Much more than an end
Herald new life in the dark
Uninterrupted

January 2022

52. Sometimes the Rage Bites Hard

Rage – noun
1. a. Violent, explosive anger.
1. b. A fit of anger.
2. Furious intensity, as of a storm or disease.
3. A burning desire; a passion.
4. A current, eagerly adopted fashion; a fad or craze.

Not 1a but maybe b,
Certainly 2, unequivocally 3
But I doubt 4, no trends will follow me

Spinning on the disco floor
To deadly grateful's long strange trip
That origins in cratered womb
Where magma sleeps, content and mellow
Counterpane of earthly crust
Waiting for its lava chance
Through boredom's pressure vents
A red hot molten avalanche

Behaved and mannered lad confused
Cocooned in web spun by the rules
Orphaned in his pupa dreams
Dated back to ancient genes
Long faded, ripped, cut short, discarded
Remnants left in double helix
That runs through mother most would doubt
Who's own sorrows buried deeper
Until dementia lifts the sod
Exposing odorous malcontent

Running in the Dark is Nuts

No six feet shallow enough to hide
The stench of rotted talent

Sixth sense in second son ensures
Corrigible in callow years
Back burner rage on rolling simmer
'Till key to door sets demons loose
Fulfilling self made prophecy
To be the one that flies this nest
A phoenix not known by his own
His water much too thick for kin
And kith, save few, who won't condone

Flowing molten lava scorches
Death and rebirth cast in one
Spinning vibes from deadly fingers
Soothing angst through unseen flows
Don't get me wrong not just the dead
The third, the man, the underground,
Good captain, Grace, McLaughlin's vishnu
And even more bizarre right now
The passing of the Perfect girl
Set these rambling thoughts in train
Rumours filling empty space
With airborne pumice stone
That scrubs and cleans barbed granite plug
Volcanic core to me
But her depart and final song
Left holes I never would foresee

All tripping moments fast and slow
Pounds, shillings, pence changed this lost soul
No home he liked to call his own
All promised lands, no milk nor honey
Just blood that ran as thin as water

Neil Garrod

Until one day he found his haven
A stave built round his futile notes
'Till score ripped up, the baton broken

Tectonic plates slip slide away
New form, new shape, new disposition
If truth be told I still don't know
Just where I am or still might be
But am amazed at where I got
Just wish with some more modesty
And comfort with my Gordian knot

Bipolar worlds, both up and down
No playing field set flat
Not knowing to or from
A joyous place to launch unchocked
A lonely place when norms impact
And asked "And where do you come from?"
Much better phrased by regal champ
"Hello, have you come far?"
You bet, but not that you would see
Its tricky for me too
Just my Dorian eye can view
That psychedelic debut

Cold turkeys roost in evening light
When pinkish shades give rosy tint
Unclear that shades of pink from past
Rekindle reds and whites so strong
In these my ageing shades
But I can see and feel and hear
And know how strong they were
And still right now they burn so bright
And fight the shade that grows each day
That never can quite quench

Those flames enkindled in drought years
By deadly marching troupe
That set the base for vivid life
Confusion and of doubt
Blowing in a wind that never knows it's port
As starboard sets its sail to unknown
Lands that shimmer in the haze of strife
Siren dreams that crown the dead as kings of life
Not knowing where to go or where the trip will end
Yet doubt does drain and energy does dissipate
As clocks click by and head and body separate
A vicious choice from god
Just like the rib that always was a second thought
And how do we make choice of apple, bone and serpent
And that greedy adamant unable to say "no"
Should we applaud him or abhor?
Should we, could we, have resisted?
I think not, so let's man up
Stop blaming her, give snakes their legs
Let Nancy keep on dreaming
But odd to me, that most of all
The apple comes out shining
Maybe that's why the authors of the book
Made it fruit of choice, just like the Newton man
A global orb, the doctors' weep, no blame ascribed at all
Or maybe it encases shame
That needs an atmosphere
To breath and grow and multiply
In sober recollection
Rotating Bob on disco floor
Throws caution to the wind
Constraints unknown as never grasped
Squashed underfoot on mini roof
In cratered obloquy

Neil Garrod

"Steady on", but hearing off
All brain cells disengaged
No limits here but no excuse
Just smouldering red hot rage
Allowed to vent on disco floor
Or mini roof
Or soaring bar strapped notes

To some with feet upon the ground
Firmly set who stand their ground
Blinkered to all common ground
Who have no ears close to the ground
Who like to cut the ground from under
"High" explains it all
But those of us that fly
Know nothing will explain to them
Why Icarus should never die

Those deadly notes, sun kissed on high
Make everything seem right
Until wax melts, we crash to ground
Our eyes now gifted sight
To see that rage misunderstood
A friend to us in doubt
Whilst future shock explains a lot
Young Alvin missed a trick
His exponential trimmed too soon
The infinite left wanting
A magic number not absolute
Of which we seem so certain
Grasping at unknowns makes firm
Solidifies our doubt
On which we stand with Heizenberg
Arms linked as we freak out

Running in the Dark is Nuts

Just like as on that long strange trip
That brings us back to earth
Once orbit has been made
That showed the darker side
This JJ stream attests and screams
The rage still runs its course
Channeled by its soaring grooves
To see that we were wrong
But wrong is right when it's been done,
No rubber for the past
That moulds our certainty unknown
The dye and die now cast

As floodgates close on past review
Reflection just too wan
But like to think it offers space
For those that walk behind
To spin their twirls in open space
In some ways good to see
In others it's so drab to know
Their joy an echoed me

 Forever further down the road
Its best to not look back
I've trod that path I've clipped those heels
Too late for other tack
Memories glow in autumn sun
A solid almanac
As still those tinkling, jarring notes
Paint vivid my soundtrack

December 2022

Neil Garrod

53. Dressed Stone

Some of us are single rocks
That don't know how to roll
Too many jagged edges
That snag on every pole

But time to time rocks do collide
Whose contours match and click
That sends reverberations deep
Through more than touch and flick

No passing crush from this impact
As fleeting kiss can linger
Penetrating through my core
To make my whole rock limber

I do not need to name you all,
Not done for pay or medal,
So few and yet you've fashioned me
To something like a pebble

March 2022

54. Friendship

Friendships laid down to age horizontal
When sometimes the vintage means vertical stance
Pick, squeeze, ferment then timely consumption
For better enjoyment, don't take a chance

Some juices immediate, no sense to preserve
Some need long storage to come to their best
Some flow continuous storage not needed
Cork, box or screw top no need to be stressed

Important to know if full bodied or light
So wine racks not cluttered with stuff that should go
Decant it or swig it, each to its own
Read closely the label, cru or nouveaux

Murky or not they're all worth a try
Dabble or plunge in, whatever your taste
Know they'll be different, your palette's your own
Some will be forgotten, some never replaced

September 2023

55. Folded Parchment

My preface written by others on air mail flimsy paper
That folds and can be posted, assisted by those others
An invalid passport to other places
Where others should be friendly but don't see me
As my inner other mirror wants to be
And makes me think again where's an other's home?

Air mail sheet designed to fold and travel just that once
No thought applied to crease and bend
To persevere in different climes
Folded in my back seat pocket
Ignored, defiled, sat on, crushed

To take its shape of me
That I myself just cannot see
Or recognise as mine but
Of the others who first set the ink
Until a new chair makes me
Feel a princess' pea
That, to large extent, reshapes that page
But still leaves fragments of the other
Dessicated memory
That keeps its meaning sourced and fixed
In one straight furrow, rut and trench
That incubated this tender arse

Don't get me wrong
I liked the view
Just not the wind
That blew me there
Abandoned with no hope until the pea
Made jump a possibility
Where starved of all that made me grow
I found that piece of broken ware
That made that parchment shape come clear

February 2023

Neil Garrod

56. Freedom

No limits, no ties, no apprehension
A positive veiled in negative shroud
Not subject to: not, none and no
Every exclusion banned from plain sight
With none so blind as those that will not see
And none so jailed as those that will not be
Confusion, confusion through infinite choice:
Free living out open, the New Hampshire way;
Free living in prison, the lifers' cliché;
Anathema to those still flying free;
Or how about nadir, the West Coast blues,
A synonym conjured by Bobby Mcgee
For nothing left to lose
How do we know quite what it means?
Don't point the finger, it just blocks the view
Of the bird staring at you who swallowed its cage

But let's take a minute
Things not all they seem
Fabritius perch has no walls or limit
The goldfinch stands open for all to see
But gossamer chain tethers to inhibit

Shark cage, pit cage, rattled cage, gilded cage
Cages of all types for different embargoes
Bars that face out and bars that face in
Bars to meet friends, bars to drown sorrows
Bars to code meaning for our special age

Running in the Dark is Nuts

Freedom a tandem, a dual toned host
Soul without body, a schism, a ghost
A body that's cramped can't think itself straight
A soul that's suppressed can't move beyond hate
Twins who are conjoined that none can divide
But we think we're surgeons, all qualified
To butcher and trade with both left intact
Ignoring the fact it's a suicide pact
Absent the one the other just dies
Freedom released to bowdlerize
But free to roam and free to ponder
Includes the right not to choose either
Content or trapped, difficult to say
Without a detailed mirror display
Showing the chains that keep us all tied
That regally sit, often inside

Bastille Day, July 2023

Neil Garrod

57. Bud, Bloom and Blossom

Some buds never open
Whither on the vine
No space to develop
They simply resign

Others full bloom
Magnificent display
That cuts off the sunlight
To others dismay

The ones that are tricky
Are those deep inside
That bloom under cover
Their own MI5

Potential protected
So full blossom too
But foliage makes separate
Their own special hue

Most you can't get to
Their thorns do protect
But some special blossoms
Let you connect

September 2023

58. Evensong

Don't praise the day before the evening
Taught, tart and trepid warning
Don't jump the gun or think its done before the very end
Yet, too often, aphorisms asymptote to hebetude:
Whose life, which day, what evening?

Days not a choice whilst evenings are, when to start or end them
Birthday cakes arrive severe, candles for the future
Deciding how to slice it up is of our own volition
But frosting of crepuscular type tempts to have and eat it:
Daylight circumcision

Why not take it as it comes, just let the day time crumble?
Seems we like to fool ourselves that we are in control
Protect ourselves, our sovereign selves, robed out in regal clout
Trimmed in ermine certitude evoked by inner weasels:
Nascent fear and doubt

We're nervous, scared and cloak ourselves in specious prescience
A shroud of rough chip choices flaked from un-planed ancient block
From which we slowly carve visage designed from our own dreaming
But all we have are blunted tools to plane and smooth physog:
Our own square edge of meaning

Neil Garrod

Planed down our block is no more real than emperor's see through clothes
Hindsight, such a flawed holdfast, lacking pith or essence
No anchor hold to stop the launch that sets the voyage in train
And also means that journey's end cannot, in truth, be found:
Close of evening's reign

So maybe best to take the point but not drive in too deep
Bits and bobs don't make a whole without a binding force
A raising agent, component B, yeast to lift our dough
Don't forget the mountain range amongst the cwms and cols:
Allegro o adagio

Haste may lead to flawed response let others jump the gun
Confusion rains down everywhere, beware the rules that try
To simplify and make us feel we've planned the perfect crime
Just let it go, there's no control, sit back and take the ride:
A day, an eve, a lifetime.

August 2023

59. Too Many Notes

The quiet embraces
The silence soothes
The nothingness ripens
Opportunity calls
Rudely and crudely
The void is aborted
Not targeted
Not formed
Chattering words
Sent forth with no map
No something to hold
Looking for grip that isn't there
But packed for some journey
Going nowhere
Not Babel yet babble
Certainly not babbling
Brooks no opposition
Torrenting across, around and through
The silent pebble bed
That's heard it before
Déja vu

April 2023

60. Muzak

Floors and floors and floors
Of flaws that you despise, no
Lift can elevate

April 2023

61. Struck Dumb

Eyes open, mouth closed
A learning state of senses
Juxtaposition

July 2023

62. Hush

Silence sometimes is
The bridge to span the void of
Deaf'ning certainty

April 2023

63. Two or One

Shades of grey remain unchristened
Limbo in the promised land
Black and white can't come together
Attraction stalled by repulsive hand
Push and pull maintain the tension
Fooling those outside the fight
Inner forces still divided
Grey no midpoint of black and white
Warring end points stand their ground
Marshalled as a captive force
Finger tips that never reach
To blend or touch or each endorse
    That all of us are two not one
    Inner battle that's never won

August 2023

64. Unrequited

Hubris or foresight?
Curtailing the future now
Before hurts requite

June 2023

65. Com'è Profondo il Mare

Our soul, not mute, does plumb its depths through words
Of colours moulding as we mature
Chameleon lizards whose changing hues
Blend the root and host to nurture nature
Each culture gifting different tones to hear
As two seas crossed by Godot claiming voice
That spoke the shades reflected in his heart
But no such varied palette for our love
One word for all: No tones, No shades, No choice
For child and parent; For lover and friend
All duly and dully the same. No tint
Allowed for passions boiling in my gut
      What fear profound dictates that single hue
      That drains the depth of fervour mine for you?

September 2021

Neil Garrod

66. Bill Got the Lyrics Right

I recall a soft soft day, the day that we met
Fruit sundae features framed in gold ringlet
Rose coloured peaches topped with berries of blue
Celestial body that glimmered like dew
Image wiped clean by Thor's high heeled feet,
Ratatat goose step made image complete
Judges fourteen of King James came to mind
Turns out got that wrong, I must have been blind
Fusion strength needed, not a desire
Simple survival to get out of mire
So good was the mask, you fooled me for years
Maybe a twin bluff that cost many tears
      But one thing is certain your smile still casts rays
      Of pure golden sunshine on my grey soft days

June 2021

67. Labour Lea

No inside out, no upside down, no actual joint between
A Möbius loop of living breath I willfully contravene
A stop, a start, a then and now, before and then its after
Hats on, hats off, as standards rise and fall to gales of laughter

Continuous becomes discrete
But with no crowning gap complete
Confusing as onlookers sing
The king is dead, long live the king

Start to finish too much to take
Without a respite, celebratory wake
Where drink is taken to console
And wet the head of what's less than whole

A lover, no lover, auld lang syne
Labour lea, deflates with time
Does she mock me or just lament
As I do daily, my life blood spent

January 2023

Neil Garrod

68. Public Transport

Me, me, me turns you, you, you in face of blame, blame, blame
An easy trick we all indulge when road gets pitted with potholes
But one that makes us both walk lame
If puddles not seen from sinkholes

Blame game not a zero sum, sucks life from both its players
Energy much better spent on filling in those holes
Don't look to bumps or four way stops and other speed naysayers
Gridlocked traffic standing still don't need no speed controls

Instead of hare and tortoise run with one just claiming glory
Let's leave the car and take the bus to travel hand in hand
The bus lane flows in measured way, time to write our story
In double hand and all joined up with neither in command

September 2023

69. Now

As dogs of war unleash, which sure they will from time to time
And rocky road of life snags wing tipped feet to taint the purest dream
Remember Now, those simpler days of you and me, no confusing mime

New paths reveal, unfold and vistas grow, some less benign
Than those once planned and don't align with chosen team
As dogs of war unleash, which sure they will from time to time

When love was trothed, in high blood too, there was but one design
No thought of marching out of step, a single guiding theme
Remember Now, those simpler days of you and me, no confusing mime

What seems like new beguiles with extra spring to jolt our rhyme
Yet only jars and queers the forming rock of high esteem
As dogs of war unleash, which sure they will from time to time

Minds eye dulled by captivating mists that proffer nothing kind
As false leads last just few small steps no longer to be seen
Remember Now, those simpler days of you and me, no confusing mime

Take breath and rest assured this cancour need not mold our rind
No reason to distort, besmirch or alter breadth and beam
As dogs of war unleash, which sure they will from time to time
Remember Now, those simpler days of you and me, no confusing mime

September 2021

70. We Two

We sit, two beasts that nuzzle close with bared
fangs yet stroll aside in quiet with no
danger knowing that our paths will never
cross, just touch and bounce to our own orbits

Sometimes we sit, hold hands and view the sunset
Sometimes we sit across and face our foe
Sometimes, always, whichever happens, the
Sun encircled leaves proclaim the dawn

And yet we've come so close that distance seems
unreal, no chasm unspanned, history
unburdened in the gorge that runs below
and quells the tinder of every challenge

September 2021

71. Touch

Touch is the trigger to soothe or excite
Language of silence, sense passed through the skin
No syntax, no grammar, so nothing sounds trite
Surface emotions felt deep down within
Hugging or holding, squeezing or stroking
All do the job, take a foot not an inch
The flesh needs to mingle, tremors evoking
Whenever its thrilling don't penny pinch
New times, old times needing repair
Withdraw it and something soft dies inside
Tears for this spilt milk, its loss is despair
No proxy, no swap will make satisfied
    Don't take it, don't lose it, don't leave me denied
    As everyone needs that touch amplified

May 2023

Neil Garrod

72. Madres Paralelas

Parallel mothers
Pass children in parallax
Curves that intersect

January 2022

73. Angus

Changes happen, but in which way
On the up or on the down?
View depends which way you're looking
From cheery smile to sullen frown

The same spot passed as different scene
The mirror doesn't catch it
How can same point seem so other
Directional hypocrite?

Because way up means second chance
Whilst down means only one
That may or not repeat itself
A single one-take run

The question is what difference does
An up run make or down
To what we do in current time
Swim or float or drown

Too often not that clear right now
But much more on reflection
Looking up not looking down
Less chance of preconception

July 2023

Neil Garrod

74. Forever Further Down the Road

I look to you from eye to eye
But only see your back
Forever further down the road

Love marches feeling side by side
But steps from back to front
Forever further down the road

The gap between becomes a moat
That has no beam to span
Forever down the road

No eye to eye, no beams or motes
Just woody tear filled orbs
Forever down the road

But arms length can be very close
And time dries out that moat
Forever further down the road

And then you fade, you're out of sight
But I am not alone
Forever down the road

As you, my new, now see my back
Receive my backward words
Forever down the road

Running in the Dark is Nuts

You and I, in syncopation
Our places now reversed
Forever further down the road

You find it strange to see my back
Don't let your marching falter
Forever down the road

Remember this, your time has come
In sadness I'm content, to know
Your back I'll never see
Forever further down your road

January 2022

Neil Garrod

75. Take Your Coat Off or You Won't Feel the Benefit

As scenes of glint and easy fill with kith and kin
That warm the soul reflecting broader view
And light the way now nights are drawing in

The pace is off, or so it seems to those still strivin'
But times of ease are frantic too
As scenes of glint and easy fill with kith and kin

With time on hand a different challenge can begin
Where what was firm seems now to lose its glue
And light the way now nights are drawing in

Talk of such can lead to sad, reminding
What is always known but never due
As scenes of glint and easy fill with kith and kin

The new perspectives: calm, no not that sin,
Consume, excite, just wondrous, wholly new
And light the way now nights are drawing in

Light refracted from a different aeon
Paints unknown worlds in brand new hue
As scenes of glint and easy fill with kith and kin
And light the way now nights are drawing in

November 2021

76. Graded Grains Make Finer Flour

Surface clean
Not all, but some, brushed under mat
To make it seem that all pristine
And set the halo so low
To burnish emperor autocrat

Where mirage views set to promote
Those that fake and simply take
They look so calm 'cos they don't try
To touch the ground where we all cry

Religion meant to lift the load
"Next time things will be better"
In the meantime they clean up
Whilst we're left holding chaliced cup

Sometimes it feels nice to be clean
So moving on not shameful
But don't forget those belly buttons
Where dirt sits from our birth
Fermenting home appraisal

June 2023

Neil Garrod

77. I'm Sorry But I Don't Apologise

I'm right you're wrong it's clear as day
I could be kind, think you're misled
Not just purposefully perverse
That said, I still can't let you off
Your wrong as wrong can be
So I can't say I'm sorry
It's just against my creed
Which is to be as clear as day
In what I think and do
No hypocrisy or self deceit
I know myself, not you.

August 2023

78. Odour of Self Righteousness

You were in the wrong
Two wrongs do not make me right
Hypocrite stench song

July 2023

79. But What Does it Mean?

All words have a meaning
Negative, positive or simply bland
Pejorative, admiring, neither or both
Just let them lead you to their promised land

Dictionaries offer some guidance, some clue
But strictly in outline, the options are few
It's only in context words fly on their own
To places not seen yet and once thought taboo

Those options affect us in quite different ways
Some authors of note slipped into new tongue
To increase precision of each separate word
Yet still the true meaning on sentences hung

Nuance delicious and so is precision
Two angle attack that meet in the middle
To give us true meaning refined in our heads
From words on the paper wrapped up in a riddle

September 2023

80. White Horses

If truth be told its always been a greasy pole
Soft clay, once adequate, now fired in certain kiln
Glazed in holy water or scientific fact
The one, belief, the other, yet an unproved inexact
Each proclaimed by infidels as OTT
One true testament, that holds all sway with zero doubt
Yet absent visas that lift the veil
To take a step beyond the pale

Frontiers set where none once were
Hard tied to riverine and mountain spine and ruler line
Where on each side the one true truth a backbone for the most devout
Calcified in prematch anthem chants
No warm up flex and stretch
All shades of grey unamed, despised, disowned
Pure orphans, all alone, no helping hand
As proving true a tricky catch, it's only false they land

As meaning bobs on endless tides that ebb and flood, just as they should,
It snags from time to time in vortex spin,
And aphorisms asymptote to hebetude
Securing feet to shifting sands
Where fear is petrified to certitude
On loose grained dunes of status quo
And sense soon drops its shadow
Where, unbaptised, the future soon will grow

Neil Garrod

Dormant buds spring into bloom as sauce flows to the mouth
A singularity of then the cyclops views as now
With paths untaken only seen by missing other eye
The source as mouth leaves current flows
Oxbowed, abandoned, spurned, rebuked
No bridge from there and then to here and now
Past single spots, that tend to nought, but look continuous
A mirage that will soon enough become ambiguous

New brews sublime not thought before or dreamt in pasts recline
Sweet nectar flows from bitter mix when tossed upon the sea
Of doubt in wretched squalls, a blind man's panoramic view
In Permanent Apprehension of all that might ensue

White horses, of no use to some in southern lands,
Free walk to many tunes composed from impure thoughts
Not certified before but built on footings of the past
From karst, or kras, through spanish steps into vienna whirl
They set the standard, flagging up the norm
That dulls right angled claim to cutting edge

Wave after wave comes crashing down
White horses hobbled, broken, no trends bucked
As hooves, light shod, misread as haven port
Not starboard beam that warns 360 round
Of hidden perils lurking just beneath
And in whose siren call, we flounder and we flail
Above the tidal waves for seventh time
Flooded with regret that buoy of inexactitude
Spurned too soon for dragging anchor's pious platitude

Fences mark a change, a pure catastrophe
The sky so blue that falls into the sea
Of what hue?
Azure, turquoise, see through?
DMZ creates no shades of grey
A firewall of animosity
But, if the truth be known
- and let's be clear that's why we're here –
All fences slice a whole
Yet sitting on them often far from lame
Exposed, alone, fair game
Lucifer's apostle soon found out
And scorned as so they should
But with no this or that
No nuance gets its caveat

Wise owls reflect in mirrored sheen
Mirror man, mirror me
Yet still, each dawn, in thoughtless nous
Return to their own house
Where commons rest and take their ease
Not caught in day to day
And close to sun the mind flies free
With everything at sea

Infinity the limit of our count, unless we add one more
No finite rank amongst this infinite word war
A helter skelter mobius braid
Of meaning's truthful marinade

December 2022

Neil Garrod

81. Rent in Pieces

How are you today?
Oh dear,
Haven't you heard?
I'm dead.

Passed away some time ago
Not sure when, not sure how
It came as a surprise to me too
But circling flies suggested something
Put it down to Indian summer embracing fall
But then I saw the frosted ground, bare trees and acid berries
And realised it was unseasonably cold
Flies coming from me
Not to me

A separation of body and spirit
The angel's share draining all
Distilled to nought on love's white heat
A putrid body still remains
A seedless husk swept up by heartless winds
The ghost has given up
Withered and died
Starved of all victuals
Starved by its core
Starved into nothing
Gone

October 2022

82. Blind Reaper

I was right, you wrong
But still it's me six feet deep
Blind reaper theme song

July 2023

83. Told You So

Just six feet under
He still can scream "I was right"
Yours was the blunder

July 2023

84. Learn to Take Yes for an Answer

How fond and sloppy can I get
When thoughts of youth infest my head

So sweet so vibrant so very close
But gone, all done, a distant post

Images live in vibrant colour
No fade to make the vision duller

Or does the mirror warp the truth
No space for wisdom just milk tooth

Truth a much more saddening view
Of what was real, no rose spec hue

No gain from looking back
No photoshop, just kodak

But current gloom can yearn for past
A bright mirage as my holdfast

Which shimmers long but fails in role
To dig me out of current hole

Past not designed to save today
But build and pave a strong causeway

To keep my head above the water
Less a mooring, more breakwater

Neil Garrod

Holding on to jagged points
That never were, just ghostly haunts

So let before spokeshave those corners
And not leave now and future mourners

Face today in real time
No outdated paradigm

The past, indeed, makes whole my soul
As ample frogs from scant tadpole

Holes in my soles firm up my feet
Old shoes and leather now obsolete

But still I hanker for peace of mind
From past chords pulling now's window blind

March 2022

85. Reverse to Reserve

Time travel imaged as something supreme
Debunked in the Wasteland where TS explained
Then, now or future each others' sibling
Mewling, competing often just quibbling
Linked through our actions, memories, dreams
No parents, no offspring just family genes

For most of creation there is only forward
Circling is closest they get to backtrack
The gear box changed that: reverse was defined
Not forwards but backwards, our choice to rewind
To something that once was but now has moved on
And then becomes now, a future bygone

Words are not rounded, their writing straight on
Meaning more tricky, a circular play
Forwards and backwards, ungodly or pious
A combo of facts, perception and bias
That means it's all relative, a personal say
That keeps us all comfy in much needled hay

Reverse or reserve a tricky dilemma
We want to move forward in light of the past
Our own feather bed that cossets in hindsight
Through pink coloured eyeware, shaded and cool
That distort by refraction what is ahead
The past is just that, not how our souls fed

September 2023

Neil Garrod

86. Bedtime Grime

Chain mail sheets soiled in sloth
Emperor's clothes as sheer as air
No warmth, no hiding, no modesty
A fog brained cloak, no honesty

But what is the choice in a shrinking world?
Horizon's mirage on four poster drapes
Nothing caste further impacts the view
Focus on d'fense, not derring-do

Don't tell my vestige there's more out there
In here the bed bugs monitor chat
Agreement and nodding lace the debate
No need for discourse, no one to berate

Then comes a right turn, or maybe it's left
The one that points upwards shrouded in mist
Not slope that slips downwards, no graft required
Easy and painless, all effort expired

How simple to turn the world on its head
A mirror view flipped on itself just the once
How weird does that feel to a soul crushed in ice
But anything's better than fool's paradise

April 2023

87. Corporate Rot

Your dream is your own, one head beats the rest
No blue sky in sight, the zzzzz's bring the zest
No external guidance, thinking all boxed
No corporate rebranding, no logo recoxed
All groups out of focus, no polling involved
Just madness and passion, no forethought to salve
No planning, no strategy, no operational plan
Performance not measured, as shit hits the fan
Still cast in the vision, that sleep tried to tame
Madness or insight, no one has claim
To guide your own earthquake, that others won't feel
So share or keep silent, it's only your deal
    No guidance or critique, no, nothing, none
    Can better your dream, a solid home run

December 2021

Neil Garrod

88. Just One for the Road

"My name is Neil and I am a racist"
AA has nailed it coining that greeting
Releasing and freeing, if that's not constraining
My tribe in me somewhere, however I balk
Pavlov reaction not given but taught
Looking in one way, no fly on the wall
To rounden the flat view of our circled kraal
Protecting, excluding, defense or attack
Invisible blinkers, a conscience highjack

April 2023

89. End of the Road

A singles ball
no one arrives
accompanied
Roads go
somewhere
so how can they end?

They can be long
they can be winding
but how can they end?

Or do they simply melt away?
icy road
watery grave

No stepping stones
no walking on water
to next yellow brick road

Green road, narrow road, minor road
trunk road, A road, B road
all just trail away

How sad
to arrive
when it's an end

Rode out
the dead horse flogged
beyond an inch of its life

September 2023

Neil Garrod

90. Indigenism

Indigent backlash
Some men against other men
No freedom for all

May 2023

91. Crescent Moon

A font to bless an unknown future
A reservoir to slake the past
Both fed by streams unknown to each
That blend to nourish home grown roots
Strong anchored in the heady flow
That builds a canopy to greet
The sun and shade the ground beneath

New branches sprout and change their form
As lifetaps into downstream pools
Profound and deep that feed the sap
That sparks and nurtures newer buds

Like lunar tide the infidel
Is called to prayer in shadow of
The crescent moon so freshly caste
More honeycomb than Pompidou
It carries beauty seldom seen
In this the land of bell not call

What rhythym do we need for life
A font to bless and launch the future
A reservoir to slake the past

October 2021

Neil Garrod

92. Journey

The start and the end
Christened parentheses
Of unbaptised journeys
No names, no pack drill
But blame all the same
As choices taken
To shame or acclaim

Absent beginning there can be no end
But when does it stop?
When I say or you?
Start pistol shoots future
Finish tape ties the past
Umbilical chord
From first thing to last

Stationery points in perpetual motion
Only the journey untouched by both
Innocent, wholesome, unsullied and pure
Tell that to the player who came number two
Or to the poet that has no first line
But kismet and choice make a powerful brew
Reality honed to all that is true

May 2023

93. Crossing Lines

Sometimes, the normal line is crossed
Sometimes, the line itself moves on
All times, the angle not quite right
All times, just too obtuse

But age impacts on parallax
And how the straight is viewed:
In gawkish youth a pixel in that solid line
Refined, rebuffed, redrawn through handsomeness mature
Withdrawn, in grotesque age, across horizons curves

I stand aghast with measured sage and ask how this can be
My land of joy and growth untamed now barred to keep me free
A deal been struck without my ken for truant parallels
But through the bars I see them leer and point at me encaged

August 2022

Neil Garrod

94. Emigré

Imagination in red corner, contra in the blue
Trained, primed and ready for daily harsh set to
Few bets are taken, the outcome secure
Early red gains soon knocked to the floor
The only way out is that of the coward
Run for the hills before being devoured
A state of no borders, no subjects, no ilk
With no promised land, no honey, no milk
A Mariner Dutchman in constant flight
Smothered by envy if moored overnight

July 2023

95. Amazing Men

Amazing men have hidden faults so deep that no one sees
All icebergs show their nine percent but not this special breed
Some flaws so low no lift can reach the depths to which they plumb
Embraced in soothing arms of admiration's leaden ease
Where sightless ego read so wrong as 20:20 vision
Until they hit titanic berg that proves they cannot see
No boards to tread they walk the plank alone and with no buoy
Some learn to float and read the stars, a choice of their volition
To finally discover that their bummock glows with light
From distant stars emitting warmth devoid from their own sun
Whose pull of gravity still strong, no faults or guilt eclipsed
But their false shadows slowly fade in ego's failing twilight
  Their gaze now feeds the eyes and speaks the truth of self respect
  That lies on home-made bed seduced in own true dialect

January 2022

Neil Garrod

96. County Down

Points and slabs and urns and crosses
In this graveyard often Celtic
Commemorating those once here
But local slant makes me ponder
Inscriptions nearly always prefaced
"Erected by"

Who does that is first response
But, as so often, first not last
Initial glance sees self promotion
More thoughtful stance sees someone cared
Naming mourner means dead still here
"Remembered by"

August 2023

97. Dangerman

Colours are bastards
Origins unwed
Numbers legitimate
Coordinate led

Rainbows show promise
And try to refine
Strict borders that sever
No space to combine

But then they run into
Each other's embrace
Blending and smudging
Values debase

Unattached numbers
Standing aloof
Decorum maintained
Opprobrium proof

Moving the comma or decimal point
Changes the locus, artful deceit,
That fractures continuous
Makes all things discrete

Neil Garrod

Colours not faithful
They blow hot and cold
Numbers more constant
Proposition controlled

But they're not all doubles
Some odd, even prime
Some looking for trouble
Some new paradigm

Two is one zero in binary land
Two bookends kept upright
By sealed volumes of doubt
Whose unopened covers keep out the light

Let's blame the victim
Let them be reviled
Sins of the parents
Christen the child

But painting by numbers
Is perfectly fine
In learning the basics
For crossing the line

September 2023

98. Sail before Steam

Stowed away amongst untold lies of youth
Cabin boy in blinded packet searching
For emerald sight of mind both kempt and couth
Devoid of pomp and circumstance

Charts and dreams lead by the nose
Full steam ahead as turbines strain to please
No view astern just route ahead that goes
Into unknown and distant seas

But stowaways have little heft
Such lack of breadth, of surface, fathom
How to flee when so bereft
Of inborn guile and natural bottom

As blue crowned eyes shed their regal hue
And grey cells pale to limpid white
The other side of truth becomes the cue
To soar and view from greater height

One hope: to come on deck
To feel the breeze and smell the sea
Check the route and effect
The simple change in how to be

Unminding skies of innocence and guilt seen through
Toffler's shock is nought to those at sea
Who realise at one fair point the slew
Of miscaste maps believed with unfound glee

Neil Garrod

When such a flow is all that's known from birth
A change of tack demanded
Not just in style or self worth
But something much more candid

Old maps do hold and lighthouse rocks and buoys
Still mark the places to be skirted in the dark
But without radar, no land ahoy
Sonar echoes bounce to Noah's Ark

Thrusting over, time to ponder
On what lost, let by, what done in lieu
Belching funnels cloud the wonder
Of all things past still left in queue

Rescinding such a messy act
Needs scenes reset and players all recast
From furnace slave to tar and jack
As steam gives way to sail and all face past

Leave the bridge and shin up rigging
Look back or forward, left or right
Verity or dreams unpicking
Crows nest offers unfettered sight

Horizon curbs surrounding view
But captain's log shows maintained progress
As rainbow shades dissolve in sepia hue
And clean new sheets adorn the dreaming mattress

Running in the Dark is Nuts

As bedding changes quarter rolls on too
The mirage that once towered over all
Is now a blank and empty space with view
Of nothing fixed, devoid of any pawl

A brand new season of harsh acceptance
Periodic elemental friends who dane
To lose their place within some bigger dance
And sit it out en route to port of sane

All bearings lost, no space where I once sat
Should I feel at sea or in my homeland?
Neither hits the spot, both stow away a rat
That tries to build its castles on pure sand

All dreams are lies when they reveal
What shade of lie? So white and pure
That they can soothe and heal
Or grubby filth we all abhor

Moulding memories gnawed by black dog
Ride high no more as snow white steeds
Stampeding through the blinding fog
Now broken not to kick and buck against past creeds

No sailor deeds truncate the open sea
Simple sense of wind and rain and tide
Enough to free the past and reveal me
Translucent but still not ready yet to hide

Neil Garrod

No need to see the path, one foot locates the next
And moves me forward, tack on tack, to hone
Me, not fighting, still perplexed and striving
For a place more honest to plant the seed sown

I used to care, not now so much
Those days of judgement are funnel bound
Now canvas soothes, more gentle touch
That makes me think that I am found

But engined boat descends with speed
It feels like sailing days a short lived creed
Until all props reverse, collision falters
Sail confirmed ascendent on the waters

December 2021

99. Harbour Lights

Rage harboured at the dying light a burning, youthful thing
That breaks its berth in darkening days caste off in growing chill;
More sense, less hope or just fatigue can take away the zing.

Horizon scoped right from the start to see where we might spring
But options trimmed as hedges grow to slowly overfill,
Rage harboured at the dying light a burning, youthful thing.

This could be seen as major cause to which the rage might cling
But choices seem less urgent now, less need to all fulfill,
More sense, less hope or just fatigue can take away the zing.

The zest of youth infuses blood that courses from hot spring,
Pure passion rules at every turn, no buttons and no frill,
Rage harboured at the dying light a burning, youthful thing.

A slowing down means time now bends with zest still in the skin
As scabs rebleed and heal afresh, new scars that past distill,
More sense, less hope or just fatigue can take away the zing.

Mock not or even scoff at what may seem like mourning ring
A ticking clock may miss a beat yet still make senses thrill.
Rage harboured at the dying light a burning, youthful thing
More sense, less hope or just fatigue can take away the zing

October 2023

100. Searching

Where's your happy place?
I'll know it when I find it
At least, that's my case

November 2023

101. Inside Out

Happy place, inside
Not out, as exothermic
No catalyst guide

November 2023

Neil Garrod

102. Morituri Te Salutant

Hermit's home
A no numbered place
Alone and on its own
On rock, on sand, in cave, in shelter
Chez lui not of concern
Furnished by all others' absence
Warmed and heated through inner toil
From weaving webs too frail and sheer
To capture naught but ingrained thought
Forged in furnace of self doubt
Shaped on anvil of no response
Dowsed in water rank and squalid
A road to nowhere or renaissance
Revelation or current stolid

Crabs side walk to shun their future
Blind spots not assumed of note
Sideways, no ways, treading water
Time to figure own anecdote
Others think they see it clear
But they don't know or feel the fear
The side steps not a straight evasion
More a direct shimmy shake
Lost in motion, no direction
Everything and all seems fake

Hermit crabs sit on rocks
Waiting for their next abode
Trading up or Pandora's box
No pattern to this hapless road
Like the hermit they are rootless
Like the crab, no forward gear
Hubris or self indecision
Stealth assassins to any seer
Until one day no shell will fit them
Quaking in their naked fear
Feeling homeless in this maelstrom
They see they've crossed their own frontier

June 2023

Neil Garrod

103. Running in the Dark

Running in the dark is nuts,
twigs, branches, leaves and stub end butts
all pave the way to random tumbles,
chipped teeth, spent rhythm and metre fumbles

She knows
She has the sense to spurn
my early morning offer
until she sees my Dawn exposed

Why am I drawn so much to her, this flirty dusky maiden
What is it in her skirts that makes the gloom this purist's haven
I ponder this as I trot and pick a path that won't explode
With all my questions, answered as she slips her mourning robe
Her hues of blue from pink to puce hint at coming glory
In different ways on different days they colour every story

Restored to sight and not just sound
the touch and smell of morning found
taste sweet upon my lips
that kiss the brow of she who
had the sense to forgo kind invite
and keep her sweet delights and warm embrace
in bed awaiting me and morning light

January 2022

Running in the Dark is Nuts

ABOUT THE AUTHOR

Neil Garrod is a lifelong academic never quite sure which way he should be facing. His mathematical background took him into financial analysis and ultimately university leadership. He has held positions around the globe. Harbouring lifelong interests in the natural world and literature he now shares his time between the Kruger National Park in South Africa and Thames-side in Chiswick, London reading, writing and watching.

He is a keen, some would say addicted, runner who progressed through marathons to ultramarathons. In 2001 he ran from Rome to Glasgow in 61 days averaging a marathon a day in celebration of the 550th anniversary of the establishment of the Univerity of Glasgow in Scotland.

He is a Welsh speaker with a mother from Aberdeen, Scotland and a father from Hellifield in the west Riding of Yorkshire. A veritable British mongrel.

Printed in Great Britain
by Amazon

ef26417b-0935-49d2-9733-5b13a2379eacR01